A Whale's Song

By Cameron Macintosh

Whales are very long
and quite wide.

They live for a long time.

Whales have fins,
but they are not fish.

A fish's skin has scales.

A whale's skin has no scales.

No scales!

A whale has flukes, which help it swim.

Sometimes, whales swim in a pod.

A pod is the name for a bunch of whales.

A whale can make up tunes to call to its mates.

This is what whales do to chat.

June and Pete like to track whales.

June makes notes on the whales.

Pete uses a pole to put a tag on this whale's back.

Then they use Pete's laptop to track the whale's trips.

CHECKING FOR MEANING

1. How are whales different from fish? *(Literal)*
2. What is a group of whales called? *(Literal)*
3. Why do you think Pete and June tag and track whales? *(Inferential)*

EXTENDING VOCABULARY

scales	What do fish scales look like? What do you think scales feel like? What is another meaning of the word *scales*?
flukes	*Flukes* is the name for a whale's tail fins. What is the base of the word *flukes*? Can you think of another meaning of the word *fluke*?
tunes	What is the base of the word *tunes*? What other word could the author have used instead of *tunes*?

MOVING BEYOND THE TEXT

1. There are lots of different types of whales. What are some whale names you can think of?
2. You learned a lot about whales in this text. What other facts do you know about whales?
3. What other animals live in the sea?
4. If you could work on or near the sea, what job would you choose? Why?

TIME TO WRITE

Write about two whale friends who meet up in the ocean. What do they do together?

PRACTICE WORDS

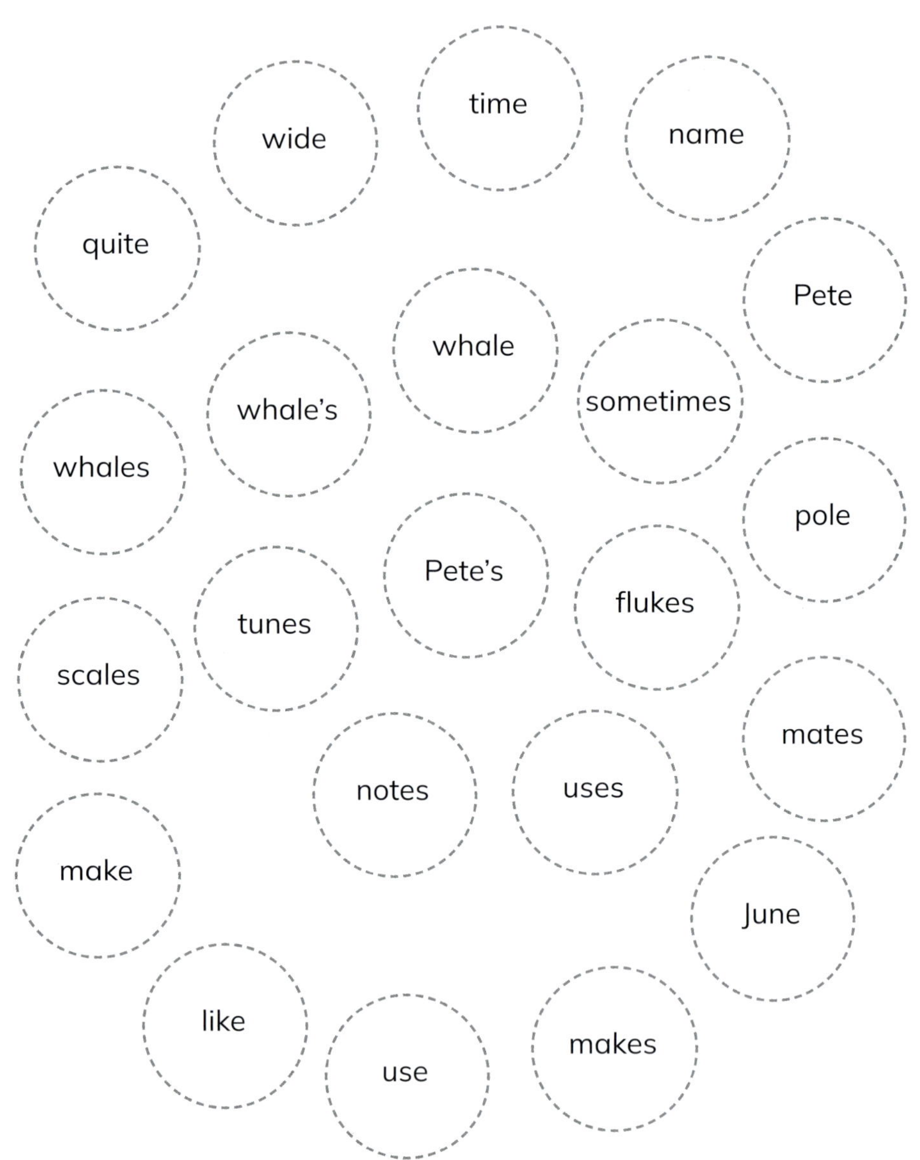